For
May 2018

Love,
ViVi & Pops

The Bluebird Run

The Bluebird Run

Poems by
Greg Keeler

2018
Elk River Books
Livingston, Montana

"His Tidings" and "Rust and Mud" were previously published in *Poems Across the Big Sky II: An Anthology of Montana Poets*, edited by Lowell Jaeger and Hannah Bissell, published by Many Voices Press, 2016.

FIRST EDITION

Published by Elk River Books, LLP
PO Box 2212
Livingston, MT 59047
ElkRiverBooks.com
press@elkriverbooks.com

International Standard Book Number: 978-0-9863040-3-3
A limited, signed and lettered hardcover edition of this book was also produced, ISBN: 978-0-9863040-4-0.

Cover art by Greg Keeler
Cover design by Megan Eubank, Eubank Creative, Inc.
Book design by Marc Beaudin

For Catherine

Acknowledgements

My thanks to Michael Sexson for reading and commenting on these things from the start, to Ricardo Sternberg for his apropos suggestions, to Beverly Voss for her compassionate ear and to Marc Beaudin and Andrea Peacock for making this book possible.

Contents

"What falls away is always. And is near."
　　　　　　　　　　　–Theodore Roethke

The Bluebird Run

Call us silly, flawed and left behind.
Call us followers of trickles gleaming
in the wind, too fickle for a made up mind,
too stubborn for a life devoid of dreaming.
We've noticed that the golden willows all
blow one way, so that's the way we're going,
and we're going on the bluebird run to Wilsall.
And if the road should run beyond our knowing,
tell the magpies, tell the hawks the wind
is in our favor. We're looking for that flash
of blue to make us new and to rescind
the winter for a while. If we seem rash,
or foolish, then assume a smile tells all,
and we're going on the bluebird run to Wilsall.

How Many Words

After a morning reading poems my mind
scampers up trees with no end in sight.
So many phases of the moon can blind
the eyes. I blink and stars emit their light
between the clouds above a Chinese lake.
Have I lived too long? This old robe
I wear winters for my body's sake
makes a good bed for my old cat. Slowed
by age, I don't know when to start or stop,
but knowing you're a gallon of gas away
keeps me listening for crows that stay atop
my neighbor's firs as snow fills up the day.
In all the flakes, how many words remain,
and how long since we've heard the sound of rain?

Enjambed

What's not enjambed I ask my friend who's seen
the leaves die all too often for a single
life. What's not cut short? What's not turned green
that seemed to end in snow? A certain tingle
in the amputee calls forth as in
a dream the sensings of a limb lopped off,
a déjà vu as former selves begin
where nothing seemed to end. The trough
of daily rituals turns radiant with
the death of one who shared them. And our lives
go on. How fair is that? Bring on the myth
of continuity—something that contrives
an afterlife for those of us who've failed
to make amends before this one's curtailed.

Just in Case

Baffled by this constant storm of light,
the mind turns dark and curls around inside
the skull. A singleness of purpose trite
as roots to any plant or word abides
no starlit corridors beyond the glaring
fact of brute intention. Why not break free
of questions and live as one intent on sharing
the homely lies desire makes of eternity?
Here among the bugs and bushes beauty
calls for a slimming down of hearts grown
fat on rainbows tucked beyond the moody
hues of cynics for whom nothing's set in stone.
For some the skull's a fine and private place—
with mouth and eyes and ears, just in case.

Hand in Hand

That we still ache for touch is no surprise.
To feel a presence or know a voice can keep
a body going till the spirit dies.
Though each of us wanders an empty sleep,
those casual moments of our waking days
when we sit hand in hand recharge our blood
with all that came before, the subtle ways
our human ties have kept us in the bud,
the fingertips, always ready to bloom
at an instant. For all else we take
for granted willingly, there's always room
for resurrections from that spark we make,
that place where our forgotten instincts thrive,
that bridge that makes us glad to be alive.

Simple Turnings

Blown away with roses and moons, the stout
answers sway in their sentences like winter trees.
In the gentle arch of your foot there's little doubt
the child was never laid to rest, the knees,
the wrists, all the simple turnings that keep
the fact of you from dwindling to a dream.
Where your ancient crystals shed their deep
light across the gulfs of sleep, a seam
of jade divides what is from what might
have been while frost etches its floral patterns
far beyond the reach of morning light.
Can you salvage meaning from these tatters
I keep making of your tapestries?
Can you abide my writing as I please?

A Bed of Grass

The clatter of stones down a riverbank
makes a happy dirge for a lost youth,
especially when nothing but the rank
smell of mud in summer can carry the truth
all the way to the present. Lying on a bluff
beneath a day moon, who wouldn't ride
a bed of grass deep into the rough
rumble of a passing train? To hide
the hurts so many cities spring on the meek
the sound of water exacts its gentle toll,
bearing pain away in breezes that speak
the subtle language of grasshoppers. Whole
lives can slip by in a doze of bees till towers
of gathering clouds wake you with soft showers.

A Belly Full of Stream

To drink from a trickle of brook I push the green,
low grass aside and see my eye and eyelash
there above the pebbles. To sample what I've seen,
I prostrate myself before the swirl and flash
of water that tastes like the purple turned blue
on the cheek of a trout. Somewhere along the way
I lost my place in a sturdy world come true
and wound up here, tracing the glimmer and sway
of weeds in a dream of summer. How black the shadows
of rocks submerged. How stunning the web the sun
makes of itself, falling from mountains and meadows
into the light of this gold and freezing run.
Splayed out on warm gravel and bursting at the seams,
one could do worse than a belly full of stream.

The River Stays

The stream flows black between its icy shelves
granting yesterday its solemn truth.
So many starry nights outdo themselves
this way, inching backwards toward our youth.
We enter some dark room and flip a switch
to exit dreams of resurrected friends.
What we've always wanted seems a glitch
in all the means neglected for our ends.
The way the clouds stand sets apart our days.
Praise to the wind and to the hidden sun!
The current slides away; the river stays.
Did you think you were the only one?
Feathers fall from a forbidden loft.
The d in death is hard; the end is soft.

At Costco

Carted off this way, we come to a nexus
called spring. When the wheels flew off, we aren't
sure, but still our valley sparkles and something infects us
with a familiar longing right down to our burnt
and frazzled nerve endings. At Costco I saw
a sparrow hopping lost down a giant aisle
among the bargain-sized boxes. Natural law
seemed to be rewriting itself as, all the while,
hair-netted matrons passed out free samples
to anyone without feathers. The terrified bird
burst into flight for fear of getting trampled,
and, suddenly a flat day gained a third
dimension. My role as a shopper narrowed
down to a fact: The air was all the sparrow's.

In Cahoots

That we might be free of trees and roots
we indenture ourselves to moon and stars
but find all elements are in cahoots.
As the breezes strum their green guitars
we squirrel away our dreams of drumming rain
and free what butterflies our memories hold
then sigh a rose upon the windowpane.
This talk of getting old is getting old.
Here's hoping that an early robin shows
to bear the burden of the season's gloom
and find an early worm among the snows
before the first precocious crocus blooms.
Till then I'll keep my thoughts of you inside
and let these fantasies remain implied.

Ample Drama

Complex allusions seem to fade with age
and back we go to dogs and kitties, cows
and chickens, glad we've kept the sense to gauge
our progress in the simple things that house
our thoughts. That's not to say the simple things
are easy. Earthworms stretched on flooded walks
can hint at meanings in a tongue that brings
us close to tears, and who doesn't balk
at a tadpole in a crawdad's claws?
What brings us to our knees in summer grass
and holds us to acknowledging our flaws
is satisfied with watching insects pass.
Let the young depart from what's at hand;
for us, there's ample drama where we stand.

Old Tunes

Disillusioned every time the sun
sets, we've come to know our bodies well,
the fabric of digestion, the nerves that run
the gamut of our waking hours, the spell
woven by one breath after another. What hope
we manage beyond the measure of our pulse
stays well within range of our ability to cope
with sorrow. Thus we dance our practical waltz
to the beat of the here and now. Old tunes the dead
taught us live in the gentle way we hold
each other. The substance of the things they said
animates our conversations till the cold
drains from our voices and an impulse stronger
than desire hones our will for living longer.

Beyond the Frost

Sometimes our bodies moan when we would sing,
a winter sound wrapped in a summer mood.
Unwrap the leaves exposing everything,
and autumn comes reciting all its crude
inflections. We look for safety in the small
sounds of spring, but songbirds drown them out
exposing us to the warming grasses, the tall
shadows of those we loved, coloring doubt
in shades of violet. Beyond the frost
I smell the sunshine in your hair across
my face and taste the berries on your lips.
Making circles like a rock that skips
across a silent lake, I'm freed from reason
following your lead into the season.

Dioramas

What is work but the blind effort of those
who would be lost in the forest's green tunnel?
Behold the fish in the shallow pool, nose
to the current, illuminated tail to the funnel
of the past. Those who wonder what can I do
need only limp into night's hidden chambers
and follow the scent of jasmine and fern through
dioramas of a previous life. What embers
are these, smoldering in the scorched thickets
where we played as children? Are we willing
to ignite our stunted desires among the crickets
that still inhabit our summer dreams, trilling
their note of caution from their chapel of grass?
Will this longing for our lost ones pass?

My Red Canoe

When I think of the water we are, my blood
starts heading for the door, tired of the boring
party nerves throw for insomnia's sake. Each thud
of my heart comes as a surprise to the warring
factions in my head. I've spent too much
of my life rowing my red canoe in circles.
Judging by the gentle way you touch
my wrist, I'd say you understand the miracles
it takes to keep us floating together down
the same river. Where the watercress
turns silver below the moving surface, we've found
safety in a pulse beyond the stress
of bad news. So, flecked with minnow thin
light, let our peaceful days begin.

Beyond Forgetting

Forget the gloomy tunes the bus radio played
across the central plains of Turkey. Just
because they all came true hasn't made
them riper for the memory. Forget the dust
and windy cliffs of Rhodes, the pastel shacks
of the Bahamas. Those seabirds that you saw
so many years ago left their tracks
and laid their eggs regardless of the law
that loneliness prescribes. Forget the bays
of Mexico where pilot whales and manta
rays breached to show themselves in ways
that stain the heart forever. Why can't a
memory ditch the pain of so many setting
suns, their colors far beyond forgetting.

Moon on Moon

Sometimes the pull of those we love who've died
makes a roiling river of our nights.
Dragged down to our dreams we must abide
by laws of those who've given up their rights.
Moon on moon surrendering our pasts
we learn to count our years among the quick
reflections of a world where nothing lasts
and lessons of the daylight seldom stick.
When morning comes and we come up for air
and gaze through windows at a morning sky
feeling just a little worse for wear,
it strikes us that perhaps we'll never die.
As foolish as this waking thought would seem,
might we persist in someone else's dream?

Puny Fonts

By what miracle we're still whole and above
ground only the gods of dormant dandelions
know. Sitting at this keyboard trying to shove
my virtual head above virtual water, I'm science
personified. Why ride this goofy machine
into the mysteries of spring, hoping beyond
hope that nothing crashes before I mean
enough that you pick up on my fond
intentions? Sleet against my window sounds
like my fingers, tapping out their brittle
tunes before a month of thunder drowns
out the last of a long winter's little
messages, pattering into puny fonts,
striving to elicit your brief response.

Sonnet

Grays
snow.
Days
blow.
Spring's
late.
Things
grate.
Your
news
cures
blues.
Present
pleasant.

Don't Ask Me When

Two Steller's jays show up, though slightly stunned,
to flutter, shine and squawk us into spring
while robins puff themselves to look rotund
and chickadees decide which song to sing.
Above, the geese and ducks come coasting home
as in the fields the cranes crank out their calls.
Crows and magpies ferret through the loam
while sleet blows in from intermittent squalls.
First cloud then sun then cloud then sun again
keep us wondering how we ought to dress.
The buds are bound to pop. Who knows when?
What happens next is anybody's guess.
I've fallen on clichés to get me through it.
I'm sorry, Sweets, the weather makes me do it.

Gravy

What are we doing here in the twenty-first
century? Don't you feel that we're always being
dragged back to the previous one with those worst
wars and all those automatic things freeing
us up for lives of leisure? Though the birds
and trees and rivers seem the same, we're
all surviving in a future we never had words
for. Did we think we'd be dead by now, clear
of the millennial quandaries in an attic
of old snapshots? But here we are, ten
years in and counting. Something's awfully static
about this stolen time, as if we're living in
the ruins of our predicted lives. Or is it
all just gravy, an extended visit?

Water and Air

Show me the factory where clouds are made,
where elephants and footballs seem at home
and objects become memories as shapes fade
into other shapes. What haven't we seen in that dome
of children's dreams? Ants line up before
the cathedral as horses become ships that carry
the moon through a vast blue ocean. Nothing more
than water and air, the war continues its prairie
blitz, blasting red megatons up the skyline
till the heart pumps a frenzy of belief
to the brain and the apocalypse dissolves in a fine
mist, shelving on the rim of the world. Brief
kingdoms collapse into a likeness of your
body, recumbent on a distant shore.

Your Riches

I see you now among the riches spread
across the floor, your fine fingers picking
as your fine eyes ferret gold from lead:
a tiny lantern, a silver watch still ticking,
a music box that plays a tune from the past,
a candleholder from before the Holocaust.
You sort these treasures knowing what will last,
what needs saving, what's already lost.
But, among them, I see only one,
long underestimated, long ignored,
and her subtle beauty leaves me stunned.
She shouldn't be neglected but adored,
so rich in history yet so set apart,
all illuminated by her heart.

Sonnet 116 Revisited

There's no stopping the marriage of true minds.
My love wouldn't change you for the world,
though the world may change. No one finds
love in a moving target. A flag unfurled
in a tempest, it holds steady and shows
the heart's true colors. Love's not Time's bitch,
though what Time does to our bodies blows.
To love, hours and weeks are a real stitch.
In truth, love will stick it out until we croak.
I'm just sayin', Shakespeare had it right,
though he was just an old-style British bloke,
and what you've read so far is Shakespeare Lite.
    If this is wrong, that limey should have quit,
    pigs have wings, and I can't write for shit.

Something Droll and Wise

I realize that you are not like her,
but she's alive in you as well as me,
and sometimes your dark laughter seems to blur
the line between the lights you each could be.
Can you imagine how she'd comment now—
upon your broken heart, my lasting grief?
She'd most likely laugh and tell us how
the world is fucked up way beyond belief.
She might suggest we pray then roll her eyes,
size us up and gently shake her head,
coming up with something droll and wise:
"I'd like to help you out, but I'm still dead."
She'd turn and leave with some sardonic oath,
that let us know she's happy for us both.

A Stubborn Beauty

For you, a slow and easy rain, not snow
where April's darkened colors hold their own.
For you, the blurry clouds pass soft and low
and budding trees assume a neutral tone.
That sorrows come head on and seldom swerve
confounds us worse on bright and sunny days.
Though nothing's in the climate we deserve,
there's solace in the weather's rainy grays.
When we heard that pair of sandhill cranes
then saw them flying low into our dreams,
their feathers were the color of the rain.
The past is not the future that it seems.
With gray, a stubborn beauty's in the air.
No wonder, friend, that I should see you there.

Town Critters

While on the trail I follow through our town,
the critters I encounter let me know
we're not the only action going down.
There's drama almost everywhere I go.
Bunnies crowd the bushes by the lawns.
Near the stockyard, whitefish pock the stream.
Whitetails graze the hillside with their fawns.
Sandhills strut the fields as in a dream.
How many eons have these creatures been
inhabiting this valley where we live?
When petty matters put us in a spin,
what solace these inhabitants can give.
In spite of human arrogance I've found
we're not the only animals around.

After Reading Too Much Whitman

Pack up the waffles and entreat the rutting bugs.
Loose and easy I snorkel the wind to my
advantage, donning a beverage for bees and thugs
alike. I've come thus far, buzzing and hooting the high
notes I require for my ambient leanings. Who tweeted
me that my coyly stropped and frazzled chest
expands with such gratitude? Please be seated,
my desolate comrade, and I will tell of the best
and the worst that unhinge me. I assume the pliant
attitude, aware that my throbbing body
needs only a firm stance. Astride the defiant
flotsam that death commands, I make no shoddy
overtures. Down to my molecules, I'm raw
and standoffish, holding only to the soul's law.

A Swan

You're in the mind of a migrating swan
in its high, cold pain over Ireland. Below,
the deep greens give way to a lake, and on
your descent, you lean on the remote
and change channels to a show where a pretty
woman has taken a mouthful of worms for money.
You walk outside where rain makes bubbles on the city
street. You see yesterday's funnies
soaking on a lawn chair. Can time have passed
so quickly? Last month your shrink asked, on a scale
from one to ten, how do you feel? At best,
you said, an eight, so he prescribed a stronger pill.
But no matter how many milligrams you take,
you know there's still a swan somewhere, and a lake.

These Greening Days

On days that green and blue muddle through
translucent leaves and petals swelled by rain,
the windows between clouds shine like they do
because of you and rays the day's long pane
lets through. Too white, too white! The snow-capped peaks
tell the long green valley what they want
to hear and the rivers pick it up in streaks
of brown and blue where quick finches taunt
each other on the breeze and a drowsy rainbow
goes on and on where sun follows the wind
toward the broad sweep of noon. The flow
I follow leads to you, riding the thinned
minutes joy allows with its secret ways
down the corridors of these greening days.

This Wrestle and Twist

When May rains soak the valley so green the river
churns brown and the cottonwoods pop their sticky
stuff on any gorged deer that passes, there's never
short shrift of worms for robins or blossoms for the tricky
business of bees. The river's bottomland
swells by the sopping pith of a rotting log
where oyster mushrooms push and crowd in a band
on their stump and morels bulge up in the grass by their bog.
Soon we'll be among this wrestle and twist
of the old and the new, plucking what flesh we can
out of these burstings forth, these fungal fists
(or better brains) that hold this daydreamed span
of days, and when we eat what they've distilled
we'll partake in what the rain has willed.

Fish

The fish I'll catch you flashes under drops
hitting water. It's colored like the storms
that never leave. You've seen it in the shops
you frequent, its subtle flash behind the norms
and fashions of a distant past, its eyes
of velvet black and gemstone. Can you feel
it swimming in your pulse, its shape, its size?
Beneath the surface, who would think it's real?
But when it leaps, the water falls away
and leaves a silver fill. Among its scales
the galaxies expire by light of day
and roses shed their petals for its gills.
Its flesh is more than we could ever know.
There's nothing we can do but let it go.

A Duck or Two

Where in the fuzzy future will we find
that bower of leaves and shadows where at last
the past relents and it's just us with our kind
intentions? In these shallows where we cast
about for reasons to get us through the day
you always spot a duck or two and make
it all worthwhile. I didn't know what to say
when you turned on the path and, in the wake
of our hopes, asked me if I'm ever happy.
Of course, I saw my answer in your face
and said so. Even in this time of snappy
comebacks, a plain response has its place.
Your common sense is what I've often lacked.
My love for you is just a matter of fact.

Fragile Days

In the strobe of light and dark, these days
slow it down to yellow blue and green.
The songbirds stopping by amend their ways
to fit what pleasures you and I have seen.
Lily of the valley claims my yard.
Cherry blossoms thrive and fill the gaps.
To tumble with the season's never hard,
but this day's final in the great perhaps.
Just to say your sorrow tastes like rain
conceals the joy your skin shows in the sun.
One day's not like another in its pain.
It's heat and cold that make the weather run.
Because despair is never far from bliss
I'll hold you close on fragile days like this.

Hang Up

What the telephone used to say by wire
it says by something else. The voices come
and, regardless of the latest mode, can inspire
the closing of a forest. A constant hum
precludes our dreams, sends mountain streams
rushing downhill toward help that never arrives.
A phone can turn a landscape to extremes
simply by playing the latest tune. What drives
us toward love doesn't always get us there.
If the songs of birds start resembling dial tones,
or vice versa, hang up. They say the air
beyond the cell towers is so clear it hones
the senses down so fine that you can hear
the childlike conversations of the deer.

Falling

To see a trout as a mutant death's head
in the shallows one needs a mind of dark
glass, a sunny afternoon and a lead
disposition. Under the cliff's stark
outline the boulders seemed freshly fallen,
and the wind was out to tell us what it meant
to be crushed. Could it have been the sullen
chair that faced the roadside cross, the scent
of plastic flowers that slowed us to a crawl
in our dream of escape? After the joke
ended, the falling seemed to stop. All
up and down the river the poison oak
was green and full of promise. Just to stand,
we had to lift each other by the hand.

Goodwill

There is so much in my house destined
for Goodwill, but I haven't the will to take
it there. The shoes, the jewelry, I can't be lessoned
in the ways these find a further use. Make
no mistake, she who once wore them wore
charity like a second skin, but it's
enough for me to make it out the door
to you. I think of how your clothing fits,
worn but not worn out, how your heat
and shape give it life beneath my hands.
Though we both be cast off, we're complete
as something new. Our present easily stands
the test of memory as our hearts are beating still.
Together we might make it to Goodwill.

For the Most Part

Someone brought the pheasants out here to shoot,
but a few of them got away—like that one there
at the edge of the road. Nature seems resolute
in the way it refuses to be natural where
people are involved. Those of us who find
ourselves weeping at television ads
haven't spent enough time resigned
to the effects of rivers. Try to imagine the fads
that wiped out the buffalo before you fix
yourself your evening drink because, after
that, things start to get fuzzy—like six
of one, a half dozen of the other. Laughter
among animals is silent for the most part.
We humans know this because we're smart.

Ouzel Mode

To watch an ouzel bob its little life
in and out of a stream is to know the way
love can harbor separate worlds where strife
between the land and water holds no sway.
To use the crystal current as a crutch
and live relaxed within the torrent's roar
we grip the facts of loss and learn how much
we gain when we approach the river's door.
To greet the sounding threats as something new
one needs to put one's heart in ouzel mode
and shrug off what the foam and boulders do
then take some respite where the water's slowed.
So knowing, we won't need to question why
we're underneath the surface or the sky.

Peonies

How deep are the peonies, plush in their steep
green vortex of leaves? The lost who planted
them, can they whisper from their long, soft sleep
the garish colors that foster our dreams? The slanted
morning light summons the ants and bees
up the hidden corridors of their longing.
The huge, soft petals droop their shadows to appease
the ghosts who inhabit the grasses, thronging
toward a music the living can only hear
when the summer breezes die. Why does the scent
strike us with such tawdry desires when a tear
of recent rain refracts a heavy pink so bent
on a stem that our future will never measure up,
my blowsy grail of memories, my fleshy cup.

Deserve

Do the flowers deserve the meadows? Do
the meadows deserve the rain? Does the rain
deserve its falling? When all the questions are through
and the timberline stops to show how vain
we are to smear the talus slopes with doubt,
I'll seek you out among the shadows and tears
and hold you by the sun-struck brook while trout
punctuate the water where it mirrors
the drooping columbine. The mind borrows
darkness from the prison of the jilted
heart where, through the bars, we name our sorrows
after those we tried to love. This tilted
axis rights itself in mountain air.
Friends deserve to find each other there.

Their Furtive Code

The mushrooms in us bulge into the night
breathing deeply in their pipes and gills,
inflating dreams to bursting with their light,
dulling hunger where their shadows spill.
They enter us through our most hidden doors
and glow within us like a bag of moons.
They leave us spinning in a mist of spores
or rising in a flock of pale balloons.
We spot them when we take our forest walks
as if we understood their furtive code
they issue as they swell upon their stalks
to put the passerby in mushroom mode.
Come, they say, we're chanterelles, boletus.
We'd be much obliged if you would eat us.

Fox

Today I saw a red fox hanging out
with some llamas. It sniffed around the sage
like I wasn't there then followed its snout
into the bushes. It didn't even stage
a retreat; it just vanished, bushy tail
and all. That's when I saw the perched hawk
down the hillside from a bend in the trail.
I slowed my pace and tried not to gawk
but it flew anyway. As grasshoppers whirred
from my path and a few crows patrolled the stubble,
I turned and headed back to town, feeling absurd
when a woman talking on a cell burst my bubble,
her black lab mouthing an orange tennis ball.
"I'm on my way," she said. "Thanks for the call."

Lapsed Flowers

Low light breaches the woods, an afterthought
slanting in the pine, across the words
the breeze trailed behind in lessons taught
by summer. Tracks in bent weeds tell of herds
moving among the hills, restless before
the rut, and we in our sleepy wanderings
follow the days down a dappled corridor
and into our longing. Who can guess the things
that turn us toward each other when the dark
says turn away? The lapsed flowers burn
in their seeds, discrete as a question mark
beneath a future of snow. We slowly learn
how wanton ways bestow our bones with all
the time in the world then lull us into fall.

Another Go

Let the winter settle in around us,
and let our years of sadness fall away.
Rejoice in all the ways that love has found us
and taught us how to live another day.
Yes, lay your weary body down beside me,
and toss your hurtful history to the wind.
I'll gladly let your gentle motion guide me
upon the lovely river of your skin.
And all I need for solace is your laughter,
and all I need for hope is in your eyes.
You turn each moment to forever after,
each sorrow to a blessing in disguise.
And though our spring be covered deep in snow,
we'll give our summer love another go.

Summer's Fool

Out my window a nuthatch walks head first
down a tree trunk making gravity a joke.
It all seems logical to me, at worst
mathematics to support a natural hoax.
That's how I walk these days from death to love
and back as blue-tailed gnats drift through the cool
air of shadows while in trees above
some yellow leaves detach. I'm summer's fool
for fall this year, and fall stays out of reach.
So tell me summer, who am I to know
these painful joyous lessons that you teach?
She who was here so clearly had to go.
She who is here I clearly hope will stay.
Could love arrange it any other way?

Rapids

Each leaf of the mountain ash against
this sapphire pool, an exclamation point
of yellow turning red through orange. Dense
moss on the rocks between makes green anoint
the trout below in the shadows they become.
Brook and rainbow say their names in colors
only when they turn to catch the sun
and the sun becomes what current follows;
thus I follow you where you flash in fear
and joy down the rapids of our fall.
Like rocks through deep water when it's clear
we see the wavering future blur then stall.
This stream is us—our path of flow and spin.
Why watch our step for fear of falling in?

Blessed Confusion

The wild strawberry leaves were so red against
the ground, I mistook them for the berries themselves.
But it was fall, and, with you, my every sense
kept confusing the day. Gunfire was bells,
chainsaws were bears, jets were the ocean, your hair
was a deer, your lips were my lips, my breath yours.
Your eyes changed as the sky changed—fair
to cloudy then cloudy to fair. By the sun-flecked shores
of a small stream, you were a vision from Yeats,
a trout turned girl with apple blossoms in
her hair: Such blessed confusion calls us mates,
more than any ledger, much more than
any religion, my gold and silver girl
my silly heart mistakes for all the world.

Sonnet

I'm writing this because I want to show
my true love how I try to write a poem.
In this tradition accents always go
at five per line before I bring them home
into a rhyme which alternates except
the couplet, which wraps up the last two lines.
When followed strictly this gets too adept,
and one hears just the meter and the rhymes.
So sometimes I'll put a bunch of unaccented syllables
around the strong ones just to make it sound
like a prosy chat in a form that seems unfulfillable
until the reader hears it read aloud.
And by the way that last rhyme's called a slant.
It's when I really want to rhyme but can't.

Agate

The scene you showed me that was set in stone,
cross-section of an agate showing where
cattle graze so stark in winter's bone,
polished, held forever frozen there—
I understand why you hold it so dear
and always view it with a sense of awe,
for nothing in your life is quite so clear
nor governed by so certain of a law.
No, your world has shifted every day
as those you love lose substance in the air
and what you count on slowly fades away
and disintegrates the more you care.
That's why, with time, I hope you'll come to know
my love is like those cattle in the snow.

Your Wound

Forgive me when I kiss your lovely scar
that bullies gave you in the woods of Butte.
It's beautiful. It's part of who you are
from when a little girl stood resolute.
I see her still, staring through her blood,
daring a cruel world to knock her down.
With nothing and no one to stem the flood,
she wouldn't be a victim of the town.
And so you weren't, and so you're not today.
You stand your ground in spite of a cruel world,
and since that scar has never gone away,
you carry that precocious little girl.
You and she comprise the reason why
I kiss that precious wound above your eye.

Bone Ditch

What a blue Easter, Love, good and bad.
The sun-warmed Bridgers and a few clouds
aimed our separate sorrows beyond the sad
reaches of our pasts, beyond the shrouds
of our thwarted intentions, out the hardened ruts
of a dirt road to the cedar ravine of a bone ditch.
Odd how the tossed bodies, dried of their guts
and stripped mostly to bones, seemed to switch
the day on bright, condensing all we'd lost
to a private *pishkun*. We held each other gently
in a small resurrection while crows crisscrossed
our path and your little dog bounded, evidently
still young in her age. None of us is bone
yet. Neither are we lost nor alone.

Rock-Bottom Days

It's about time the cottonwoods
budded their sticky purple wings to the fresh
air down from the powdered peaks and their hood
of cerulean sky. Here's to the river in its mesh
of early hatches, whether goslings or flies
or rainbows on their beds, whether pool
or rapid, still or white water. The size
of the season sends distant rain to school
down the long valley where it learns to be snow.
And here's to the rock-bottom days that precede
the high water, the ospreys and eagles that flow
between river and wind. The clouds only need
sky to build and scatter their will from the west.
You and I, friend, we'll take care of the rest.

Wild Asparagus

It's time for wild asparagus in May
when shoots come green in clouds of caddis flies
beneath the rubble of another day,
such vivid life betraying death's disguise.
White near roots then green to purple tips,
they suck up showers then firm them into stalks.
To pick and hold them fresh against our lips
gives form and substance to our river walks.
When I'm with you, I feel somewhat like them
among the rose hips, hidden in a blush.
I'm all awash with spring from stern to stem,
a turgid stripling rising from the brush.
It's a little bit like striking gold
or forgetting briefly that I'm old.

This Day and You

The path was full of sunning bunnies still
between the summer flotsam, motes of gold
on green and gnats in sunbeams with the trill
of finches stitching breeze to breeze the old
and simple songs of morning. All I had
to do was breathe and think of you, my friend,
the seamless way you blend into the glad
and willing sky. I walked until the end
of sorrow, past the city toward a field
of fawns in flowers blending in the mood
your steady rhythms set. In all that's healed,
the weather settles. Breezes say include,
include, and so I do, this day and you,
this sunlit tapestry of green and blue.

Carpe What?

Here there'll be no cosmic last resort,
no looming fate, no cringe inducing frost.
If I write of death, feel free to snort
or snicker when I mark the time we've lost.
Forget that old cliché of *carpe diem.*
We've seized one day; no doubt we'll seize another.
As years go by, we'll call 'em as we see 'em.
Living in the present tends to smother
the longing we invest in hopes and dreams.
Why not put off rolling in the clover?
The future keeps us bursting at the seams.
The present's really swell, but then it's over.
And what's so wrong with dwelling on the past?
As I recall, we really had a blast.

Malarkey

Here it is, laid out in five beat lines,
swelling in the form like rising yeast.
This fool who's finding words shows all the signs
he lacks direction, what a smarmy beast.
Decisions—who does that in lieu of rhymes?
He tried to make one once; look where it got him.
In truth, he might be in for better times
if he pulled his head out of his bottom.
See him pour himself a little drink.
See him poke around on the remote.
He'll find a show so he won't have to think.
See him eat the Frito, see him bloat.
See him wander toward extended care
cold and shaking in his underwear.

Slides and Swings

The slides and swings we put our children on
put them in touch with what they can't control,
a rush of air, a world that's here and gone,
a parting from that calm that makes us whole.
And as the summer trees lay down their shade
in vague, nostalgic patterns on the park
we contemplate decisions we have made
swinging as we do from dark to dark.
What once translated terror into fun,
the sudden burst of speed, the spin of heights,
somehow gets intertwined with all we've done
and makes a daunting playground of our nights
where fortune sends us whizzing toward the ground
without a gentle hand to slow us down.

Ripples

Is time the heart's dying? I wave to the waves
for your sake, my sparkling darling who knows
where the moon went. Your patience saves
the rain to lave my restless nights. What goes
on in the river's heart pulls my blood, too.
Who picked up this stone to stem my grieving? How
does the same sky survive the wounds of its blue
churning? I walk to the edge of the light and bow
down to my shadow in hopes that the present will show
up in the past, but for all the dust the earth
kicks up in its turning, the wind says there's no
going back on the promises made at birth.
This stone sends its ripples, again and again,
and once more you've borne with me my friend.

At the Edge of Your Skin

Praise to the logic of leaves, Love. Why
should I be alive? Crippled in the wake of thunder,
the rain said not yet. Better to kiss than to die.
The cows are nearby with their thud and snuffle, under
the trees for shade. The grasses hiss a song
beneath the wings of insects, and all I can do
is listen. A dead shrew on the path is wrong
for the light. The clods are how I know. Who
planted a flag in this field? You'd better not ask
the wind. When I stop at the edge of your skin, birds
too small for their songs come alive. They bask
in the scent of geraniums after hail. My words
mean little in lieu of the way you touch your tongue
to mine. Who'd guess these leaves were so young?

Blackbird

Blackbird in the rain, are you that hole
the night left in the fabric of the day?
Through the glass I hear your voice cajole
the colors from beyond a sky of gray.
Are the lyrics all about you,
or do they praise your other in the light?
Does she hear your music coming through
the branches from your little patch of night?
Somewhere among the secrets of the rain
a story's told of rights commending wrongs,
and though my sleepless nights leave me half sane
I hear the telling twisted in your songs.
When I approach the gist of what you say,
you spread your wings and fade into the day.

A Changing Leaf

Tired of seasons posed against the end,
the cycles brought to bear on skin and bone?
Perhaps I cling to adages, my friend,
alternatives to her who died alone.
How to pass the days the nights betray.
She wrote, "I hardly ever enjoyed my life,"
regardless I was with her every day
behind the calm façade of man and wife.
And what does my attention mean to you
who live alone beyond your years of grief?
Perhaps the damage that such questions do
finds reparation in a changing leaf.
Our thoughts dissolve in what our senses find.
I need to hold you for my peace of mind.

Shadows

When John Bozeman decided to make this valley
into real estate, I wonder if the magpies
acted like they do now? If we rally
all of our senses and watch the mayflies
pass through beams of light near Bozeman Creek,
perhaps the gusts from passing cars will stir
them just enough to show us how the meek
prosper at the expense of arrogance. Were
you and I such fragile beings once?
How strange that we still hear the voices
of our children playing when memory shunts
off true successes in favor of practical choices.
More and more we're shadows in this town;
I even hesitate to write this down.

Statuesque

Squirrels and deer decided to occupy
the graveyard today, standing stone still
among the stones when I passed. Die
we all must, but by what stretch of the will
do we reckon our ties to the angels and Savior
gracing those graves? The deer looked carved, too,
but seemed more apropos with their deer-like behavior.
I'd say statuesque, but the squirrels, true
to form, blew it in a frantic scamper with pinecones
in tow, so the deer blew it too, waving their tails
like white flags of surrender past Johnson and Jones,
Parker and Harris, proving eternity pales
when held up to the present. Those who brood
take a back seat to those who are looking for food.

Lively Music

Can I help it if my fantasies lie fried
in deep fat? Crusted with hot, crisp batter
living hells turn heaven, and all that's died
stays firm for that nostalgic brimming platter
of body turned soul food. From the kitchen I slam
the screen door out into the broad fields
where rabbits and chickens jostle to cram
all their bold and golden world yields
into Grandma's frying pan. The crackle
of skin and fat, salted and peppered beyond
our prudent lives, gracing the tabernacle's
potluck nights, accompanies our fond
memories of youth and begging dogs
with lively music while our hearts get clogged.

A Strict Departure

What's wild sprints away at our first footfall,
but even that is no excuse for the way
we accept domesticity. Seasons stall
for the cranes' long flight. No matter how we pray,
dragonflies trail tiny storms toward
a chaos none of us recognizes. A strict
departure from the rules finds its lord
in every dream that we forget. Tricked
out in plants and animals, we go about
our business as if we were something more
than thinking bags of water. Who can doubt
our motives considering our contrived lore,
our singleness of purpose, our great appetite,
our cities that glow like viruses in the night?

Paper After Paper

Drink just didn't seem to do the trick
any more. The racket of bottles piling
up became, over time, a sort of sick
hymn to the Greatest Generation. Styling
their voices after those on the silver screen,
they tapped the ashes off of their big cigars
and challenged their puzzled offspring to come clean.
Snapped into their girdles, women became the stars
of washing machine ads while the dog brought paper
after paper until, well, here we are, sitting
ourselves to death and hiding from the neighbor.
No wonder our politicians aren't admitting
Jesus to their ranks or paying the bills.
How can they think over the rattle of pills?

In the Precincts of Sleep

The uncomfortable meeting of mind and fact
is suddenly trussed up in the one-on-one
that saves us from what we've always lacked
in confronting mornings like this. Nothing's done
intentionally in the precincts of sleep,
yet sleep we must while all the marginalia
that quell our meetings in broad daylight seep
through the cracks of our inevitable failure,
and, voila, we're happy. Bugs no longer bite
and insults no longer sting. If someone tells
us to have a nice day, we think of last night,
the intimate sighs we heard beyond the bells
and whistles worn traditions lavish on death.
We sense the moment on each other's breath.

Mites

To start with ear or trigger or coin leaves
a gap in the trees and signals something less
than the lamp would illuminate. The eves
drip icicles straight into childhood, and, yes,
twilight grapples with the twigs to tint
clouds pinker than the songs of the few birds
left to do business in their winter stint.
No telling what will trigger certain words
when the hand is writing for money. Love
is another story. As the shadows stretch
their inklings of substance, giving the light a shove
toward recognition, hope starts to fetch
meaning, even as mites in the frozen fens
survive without the impediment of sense.

Huh?

To expunge the doings of the pilot light
we welcome darkness for its own sake.
Costly rivers with their currency of night
carry their luminous trout in the wake
of gas exploration so cars we've driven
for years sparkle under a new coat of wax.
When we plan our honeymoon, given
the attitudes of those who aim to tax
our American Dream, which small island shall
we shoot for, huh? Will the hollyhocks
our jet spews be acceptable to the gal
who makes a joke of us while cleaning clocks
at the beauty parlor or whatever it's called
these days? Will our offspring be appalled?

Blue Suede Shoes

I was going to reconstitute
myself as a singing ghost, but the samples the lab
requested left no room for my resolute
intentions, so you and I took a cab
from one dreamscape to another, all
the while singing "Blue Suede Shoes" and throwing
rose petals out the windows. Wall
after wall of graffiti inspired a growing
sense of lassitude in both of us
so we took off our sandals and waded
in a downtown fountain until the bus
to our hotel arrived. Though the memory's faded,
I can still picture us near that taco stand
dancing to that mariachi band.

Freelancing

Frog-eyed and tipsy, the shadow cleavers rant
on from their televised portals while out here
in the realm of water and wind we mark the scant
leavings of the small lives ousted by a general fear,
the logic of hoofprints in snow, news of our battered
kin freelancing out on the verge of the world.
Versed in the art of the disconnect, the scattered
functionaries tend what hopes they've squirreled
away in the long yawn prescriptions have made
of their future. Just because they've slammed the door
on a sea of carnations doesn't mean we have to fade
like that, too. We'll make our snow angels on the floor
of the forest well beyond the range of their phones,
finding our past in the river, our future in stones.

Lost Tribes

Here's to the clear in streams, the opulent eye
of reflected moons, the crowded bird-strewn wind,
all things transparent in their passing. Why
dwell on electric fantasies and rescind
our claim to the suck and lap of waves like sex?
Seen from above, do the dots we make relieve
the landscape of our need to know what's next?
The air between us turns to glass when we heave
our heavy sighs and yearn for the clench we feel
at another's touch. The furrowed fields stretch
away from our town, fanning the past to conceal
the glow in the bones of lost tribes. We etch
our skins with the wrinkles sorrow demands
and map our misgivings on the backs of our hands.

A Trace

Passed down through pearls and lockets, the touch
of those who came before eases the surface
of the past into our own time. No such
loss takes place on the face of the new. Purpose
robs artifice of its intended charm.
The boy and girl that we once were still live
in the only dimensions a mirror can offer.
Our caresses ask the dead to forgive
us, but, flattened to a page, they suffer
our longing in silence. The artifacts we pass
between us carry a trace of hands that knew
the strictures of love by heart. The cut glass
figurines are more than prisms under the blue
windows of our long and sun-warmed youth.
Who's to say that touch can't hold the truth?

All the Way Home

You never can get back. What a hollow
phrase for those who still go there. Mink
in the mountains hump their long bodies to follow
deadfall streamside for miles. Best not to think
how some folks out of habit take the easy
road home as whole forests whistle by.
Novices call the summer river lazy,
but how many souls does it take from its high
bed of needles and ferns to the concrete heart
of the city? I've seen you, friend, patrolling the rim
of your known world while clouds fly apart
and scatter down the sky to that blue hymn
the wind plays for pilgrims who go it alone.
And I would be with you, all the way home.

No Small Miracle

If you come with me across this field,
words the only birds in a land of blowing
snow, will you still carry your love sealed
in the pain-proof locket you earned without knowing
exactly why? The silences in our song
are proof of the many empty rooms we've entered
in our search for company. These long
years later we finally meet in a setting centered
on our common ground: How tall the pines!
How soft the forest floor! These brilliant monkey
flowers are no small miracle, nor columbine
nor glassy stream with golden flecks among the
pebbles. We've been here before and no doubt
we'll return in terms we've yet to figure out.

Free as Clams

Are we happy in our way of life?
The streets keep stretching away toward more of the same.
Husband after husband, wife after wife
drift into these solitary pools as tame
as shadows under these perfect little trees.
Attenuated hopes lead to this tiny
door, and, yes, it's open! Hear the sea's
shush. See the hand with its shiny
ring pull down the shade to leave us out
here in the dark, free as clams. Sleeping
clams. Were we possessed of a bit more clout,
these dreams might turn to tidal pools—in keeping
with the whims of geological time
at the behest of a species in its prime.

The Secret Word

Living in the moment trees don't regret
their roots or leaves, but who the hell would want
to be a tree? Want—is that the secret
word? The time we spend recalling the gaunt
branches of our families might just as well
be spent in each other's arms. Woodland
creatures that we are, I'm sure some swell
cycle revolves in our genes beyond the hoodlum
chickadees and other troublemakers
that stick it out no matter what the season.
Ignore the pleas of those fuzzy little takers
that mark your yard as if it were an Elysium
of seeds among the prints of little feet.
Friend, regret is just a word to us elite.

Bubbles

Call the blue and lazy loops of afternoon
something besides what they are: a father
chasing butterflies, a daylight moon
rising to meet the sun. It's such a bother
to think this way, as if the conversation
rose in bubbles with nothing but air inside
and between. Spend your whole vacation
rescuing fallen birds if you must, but I'd
do it in secret if I were you. Chatter
of this sort falls short of imitating life,
and sound advice eventually fails to matter
in churning worlds of ebb and flow, rife
with the possibility of dead birds
and the incapacity of words.

In Case

What do you know; the fox has managed to sell
himself short again, snuffling the sage
tips for no apparent reason. Well
past the city limits, we make a cage
of our hands to catch the moon this one last time,
hoping the open spaces don't fill up
with more suburban dreams. We clean the grime
from under our nails in case the world might stop
forgetting us like weeds forget asphalt
or pigeons forget barns. To say that I have grown
close to you is to admit that my gestalt
depends on the lazy symmetry I've known
in butterflies whose wings perk up then stall
when summer shows the first degrees of fall.

Grottos

Our winter walks well below the pine-high
hills and through the snow keep us moving
past the solstice no matter how we tie
our shoes in that long dark day. Improving
as we go, the trails freeze and thaw
to keep our footsteps fresh and let us know
the many layers it took to form the law
that got us here. What makes the days so slow,
the nights so long blends them all together
so the months and years speed by propelled
by a gray sameness in the wind and weather.
In those little grottos where we've held
each other to still the clock, we've held our ground
for love to slow the whirling planet down.

Pleasant Valley

We keep walking in this pleasant valley
though at times it becomes not so pleasant.
Creek beds assign blame as we sally
forth through the fragrant grasses. Isn't
that the same waterfall we passed
before the dead stole our childlike sense
of wonder? Come to think of it, the last
time I saw you, we couldn't talk for the dense
rapids of our uphill struggle. Years
ago, neither of us saw these coming:
the sound of that forest breeze that brought us to tears,
the way the evening star led us to slumming,
the magpie that taught you how to be stubborn, the daisy
that taught me how to be both plain and lazy.

A Mish-Mash

Just as carp comb the summer eddy,
their orange lips an encumbrance to the reflections
requisite for peace, we seek the ready-
made conclusions that dice our days to sections
and loll in a mish-mash of shattered ideals.
For all the Latinate constructions it takes
to confuse the issue, you'd think the squeals
of a dying pig might hold more water. Sakes
alive! What would Grandpappy say if he saw
me pirouetting through the chicken yard
in my cap and gown? Nothing's quite as raw
as language made intentionally hard—
or a book in the hands of a bumpkin, so look sharp,
all you pseudo-intellectual carp.

Days of Repetition

I try to welcome you on these launchings-forth
though the tunnels through which we worm
become narrower and narrower so our north
gets lost in the darkening walls and no firm
logic underpins our path. By
the by, your presence makes it all worthwhile,
the memories of our stint under the sky,
the way you grasped the meanings with such style
and purpose. In these days of repetition,
we've a certain eternal return to grace
so, despite my seeming contradictions,
we've come upon a peaceful resting place
where we become accustomed to the night,
while up ahead we glimpse that spot of light.

Such Jive

What the wind kicks up these winter days,
forms a haze on the summer mind. Fresh tracks
in the snow covered in more snow that stays
stray beyond a yard of frozen facts,
dance to a song written in the roots
of dandelions. It goes like this: "I'll
remember you, my love, your greening shoots,
the promise of your leaves, your golden smile."
Allowing winter won't allow such jive,
I scan the backs of hands grown old and see
a scar I made on broken glass at five.
How profuse and red my blood could be!
Regardless of the day, our hearts still know
that fresh and greening beat beneath the snow.

Summer Dreams

Standing on our roofs with the slight fear
that comes with heights, might we not sense the summer
breeze with more intensity? We hear
each other breathing sometimes in the glimmer
of light from a winter window and our lives
seem to rise from the bed to the ceiling,
leaving our tired bodies to a hum that revives
us slowly from our dreams. While we're healing
from the long day's labors, do thoughts of falling
make us vulnerable to those we love?
When morning comes too soon and we're hauling
ourselves up into the daylight above,
dripping with sleep and crippled by the clock,
will our summer dreams survive the shock?

Lazy Rain

We don't just fish for trout; we mine for them.
Diamond bright, the light accumulates
from stars, shines from caves that hem
the undercut. A certain moment waits
for us, cloaked in the finery of fall's impulse,
sheer appetite disguised as love in the eye's
clear depth. Who would dare to fling the false
truths of feather and steel to win a prize
as quick and fickle as water? Should we weigh
our dreams, plumb the brook's cauldron beneath
the sudden roil where current is wind and play
a piece of stream until it hangs by its teeth
then flops on the grass, a miracle of lazy rain
fallen from such loss, risen to such gain?

Much Less Sane

When that big bunny, the sun, tumbles my way,
no telling what fat birds will show up
to puckishly perch on the grandstand firs today.
Imagining those times when I was just a pup,
I try to romp to match the mood of things,
but, golly, the brittle sticks that hold my clothes
won't even do for legs, much less for wings.
When that round piggy the moon lights up my pose,
no telling what lame ducks will wobble into view
and plop themselves down with a porcine sigh.
Recollecting those days when all was new,
I try to quack as they come limping by,
but, lordy, that wrung out sponge that was my brain
can't even keep me alert, much less sane.

Blurry Days

No transparency has ever hardened
us before. The promise of all those globes
of dew, the sun behind a wave burdened
with the wind's travails, the trailing robes
of rain falling gray from distant clouds.
Perhaps the weather can contain our doubt
though you and I are familiar with the crowds
who casually turn the horizon inside out
and jostle to confront us one-on-one.
A certain broadening settles on our lives
when tragedy assumes the role of fun
and the laughter starts before the joke arrives
trembling at some predetermined locus
while all our blurry days fall into focus.

Ironing

It was a time when everything became
accessible: the new moon, the old moon
and all of the moons in between. Blame
was never couched in the subtle tunes
of inflection, and praise lay like snow
shaped by the surfaces of our accomplishments.
"Ironing" eventually replaced "irony," so
double meanings were flattened to common sense
then folded and put away for appropriate occasions.
Stripped of our flimflam artists and double-dealers,
we knew what was what in conversations
that proved as efficient as ants touching feelers.
Nobody got laughed at, for there was no laughter.
Thus we all lived, happily ever after.

True to Form

Wha—what happened? That logging road winding
down through light and shadow bears a fragment
of our past, but daily I keep finding
newer and brighter spectacles in the pageant
time puts on for us. While the dead
converse freely in our voices, new
paths keep opening in our neurons. We've read
the birds and flowers and trees their rights, and true
to form, they've followed their better judgment home
by the lantern of their instincts. Was that us,
 that single shadow among the pines, that sum
of what we were and are beyond the fuss
of urban rituals? Why question the sun,
that early summer light that made us one?

A Fair Account

This gentle snow that makes the sparrows fat
achieves a neater pattern on the air
than humdrum summer conjures with its flat
out parsing of the way we see. A fair
account of distance rectifies the moving
flakes and freezes all that's still into
a memory fit for warmer weather, proving
the moment so often rests on motions new
with every shift of wind. And so I think
of us and how our colors fade this time
of year, our gaudy hopes ordained to sink
below a stern and structured pantomime
arrayed in black and white. That's not to say
I'd want to live it any other way.

Less and Less

Where in the face of the great gray rain did we come
to that understanding we achieved free of rooms
in a wind that opened us to the sad hum
of wires on the plain? When the drops resume
their kissing, will the clouds' expression change
with the scent of sage across spring's purple curtain?
How long have we been lost to the strange
cloud shadows our clumsy youth made certain
in snapshots we took in the wake of a simple past?
Now that we leave the highway less and less
and travel with the windows up, how fast
the scenery flies, how strong our need to confess
our loneliness—but down the road we go
fiddling with the dials on the radio.

Burning Bridges

Why shouldn't climate and our dreams be equal?
The university's recorded chimes
pierce the winter, anticipate their sequel
in an hourly procession to dice time's
general rush while in surrounding hills
cougars tackle the problems of a stern season.
Though we've acquired a certain set of skills
to insulate ourselves from social treason,
something in our pulse rings worn-out ditties
down the starlit corridors of sleep
as if our lives were drawn up by committees
with a thousand promises to keep.
Thus our dreams are warmed by burning bridges
while the big cats lope along the ridges.

Not Ready for Show Biz

Which god directed these leaves to stay on top
of the snow? Some fancy pants no doubt, some miffed
functionary who decided to drop
his work in midseason to create a rift
in the placid plain of our expectations. That
the ice on Mars might hold life packs
less punch than the detritus woven into the flat
surfaces we make in our blue routines, the facts
of our magpie-ridden winters. You out there,
you and your lovely bubble of attention, is
it worth dragging this poem out of its lair,
when, obviously, it's not ready for show biz?
I mean really, magpies, pants and Mars?
Why not trumpets, pinecones, bugs, cigars?

New Ground

As the poem breaks new ground, what's
turned up in the brilliant folds? Surely not
gold, not the old ifs ands or buts
thinly disguised as that fallow plot
the masters farmed with their colossal
plows. There seem to be plenty of worms
exposed, writhing their lives between a fossil
or two. Perhaps the poem's come to terms
with the fact that nothing's new, but that doesn't
stop it. See the fecund little rows
break up the shiny page. See what wasn't
there before gain substance as it grows
into a mighty field. Or is it chicken scratch
here on this depleted little patch?

My Little Corner

Here's another corner into which I've painted
myself as you watch from your doorway to another
room. With each stroke I'm more acquainted
with the voices of beloved ghosts who smother
my longing for an exit. To live inside this box
I must become accustomed to the syntax
of the thwarted, a certain take on things that mocks
freedom as it vanishes. The impulse to wax
eloquent dies down in the busy sound
of the brush until I'm here with my back against
two walls. It's no use to dream I've found
an exit from my prison of common sense.
In the end I'll be my only mourner,
stuck forever in my little corner.

A Last Resort

Is it enough to go on singing, to yodel
the notes across wide winter's subtle sky?
The tune's so old the birds yearn for a total
silence but mouth the dim words anyway.
When the flat hum of nothing undermines
that original hullabaloo and rabbits
shuffle through the snow between the lines
of melodies yet to be composed, what habits
will we reenact to keep us young?
Though my voice is frayed and music seems
a last resort to keep our spirits going
I'll croak a tune for you in wild phonemes
and practice my pathetic shuck and jive
until those longer, warmer days arrive.

Some Like Me

How to put to use these constant winds—
perhaps to slam the doors on all that's wild,
to drive the littles deep within their dens,
or scatter dormant seeds out of their mild
corners in the howl of something new.
Whitman did it over and over again,
but then again, before the man was through
you could only hear the sound of wind.
Poets feeling trapped revert to birds
who live and breathe and ride the wind with ease
and make their points with acts instead of words
and act as if they're doing as they please.
Thus some like me put wind in chains and locks
and try to make it blow inside a box.

His Tidings

The great blue heron is hardly blue though great—
more the color of distant rain, cranking
his call from rookeries where his mate
sits atop the cottonwoods. Banking
the winds or stalking the shore in brief sightings
from north to deep south, he carries his load
of hope for us who've learned to trace his tidings
of a deeper life. We follow a river road
to keep our lives in tune with his where swallows
flare and minnows leave their tiny wakes
in shallows still enough to let us follow
his reflection into the cattail brakes.
There like a statue he fades by the river's seams
into a summer night of silence and dreams.

Hit and Miss

Waiting here for a strike, I hold the line
in my fingers ready for a hint, a clue
to come impossible from the water's shine.
When I return skunked, as many do,
I'll bring the day at least with its mess
of reflections home to the table and you.
If we just sit quietly will you think less
of the silence I found trailing down the blue
dome and into the reaches of the afternoon?
Could it be that failure is its own
reward, that, but for silence, any tune
would dwindle to a hum, a monotone?
Would you mind if I brought you only this
from my little pool of hit and miss?

Volunteers

Another spring brings violets to my yard,
and I'm still here to bear their weight of loss.
They seem to show when I've let down my guard
poking up among the grass and moss.
They constellate, for better or for worse,
a patch of time that goes back forty years
and mark the borders of a universe,
my bedraggled band of volunteers.
Best not to think about what they outlast.
Better to regard them as they are.
Soon enough they'll punctuate the vast
recesses with their purple *au revoir*,
so ditch the past and future for today:
Pick a few and make a bright bouquet.

A Valid Purpose

They have all been put here for a purpose:
the bowling pin, the penis, the Buick, the pig.
Even when there seems to be a surplus
of, say, snowflakes, they're all part of some big
plan. Why, just the other day I came
across a mushroom shaped like a tuba. "What next?"
I said aloud, but the cancer in me remained
silent. Sometimes babies look perplexed
when confronted with their own fingers.
I know the feeling. Bend down and touch
the ground. Notice how the posture lingers.
Before long, you're going to need a crutch
to illustrate your vulnerability.
And that's a valid purpose. Take it from me.

Bit by Bit

Someone has to put a stop to it,
the way the words get in the way of wind,
stifling the small hope that, bit by bit,
we garner from open landscapes that end
when we think. Cattails, blackbirds and a sky
of songs get relegated to a back
burner in the art of texting. Why
bother with all those little breaths when black
is just a pattern of letters sent from God
knows where? Hunched over a device with thumbs
going like crazy, the pilgrim gives ego the nod
and settles for a destination that comes
with every human skull. What's important?
Who cares as long as it gets shortened?

A Casual Act

In the cool of the morning when every noise
that drifts through my screen carries its share
of a long summer story, I strain to hear that voice
between the breezes, the one that tells me where
the dead survive. It's a casual act,
the sorting out of souls, a bit like laundry
to a mind that takes birds for a fact,
their fading calls, the way they shape their sundry
music to fit some daily sorrow. Choosing to live,
I often inhabit the ghost of a former self,
inspecting my body for the same old scars,
coming across a trauma on a closet shelf.
We take the lost for granted like the stars
in broad daylight, permanent yet out of sight,
waiting there to dominate the night.

As It Is

Where does the onus belong? A woman in funny
pants keeps walking by my house. A few
miles away bison live in a sunny
rendition of some rich crank's dream come true.
While big gray grasshoppers keep flying back
to the path in front of me, I try not to think
of this as an inland sea which is now on track
to becoming an inland sea again. Why sink
into geological time just to avoid
gaucho pants? If it weren't for their wings
I'd be tempted to call the grasshoppers droids,
but as it is, there are too many things
that can go wrong. Two dimensions are just fine
by me. If you disagree, get in line.

Weeds

Grasshoppers whir up like gifts, red
then black then yellow, turning the trail
into mild fireworks, taking what's said
by light and shadow, transforming the brail
of footsteps across the meadow into a mix
more palpable than any one sense can define.
A yellow butterfly's proboscis sticks
in a purple thistle below the subtle whine
of several dozen bees buzzing up a storm
as drought thins wildflowers down to a few
hardy weeds. The party's over; it's back to the norm.
Since we frittered away the showers, all that new
green has shrunk to beige in the rattle of seeds
ready to fill another season's needs.

Our Last God

God, bless America. And if you don't,
you'll meet the same plight as others who fail to obey
our commands. That's right, we'll abandon you. We won't
stand for a weak god who doesn't play
by our rules. That's our last god hanging on
the cross, looking as if he were alive. We call
that piece a wonder, now. The soldiers' hands
worked busily a day and there he stands
(or hangs in this rendition). Some say he's gone
on to bigger and better things, but for all
the hoopla, he's probably just flat gone. So bless
this our war, our pride, our stuff, our success.
And if, by chance, your holy blessing fails
to meet our needs, break out the cross and nails.

Down

I'd never noticed how the leaves detach.
Falling windless in a morning's frost,
they indicate a world where things don't match,
where all that's gained turns into all that's lost.
I'd like to dash around and put them back,
to reconnect them like they were at first,
a film run backward following exact
patterns reconstructed in reverse.
But there they are, irreparable and down,
leaving me no choice but to accept
the way they wind up scattered on the ground,
regardless of the fools who've prayed and wept.
At best I'll only rake them in a pile
as if I might control them for a while.

Substance

How many of us are there living alone,
the clink of a spoon in a cereal bowl the only
conversation, the shift of a chair, the groan
of a rafter? This wasn't in the plan, this lonely
stint among the ghosts of remembered rifts:
Oh yes I did. Oh no you didn't—
just enough to conjure a voice that sifts
through the years and settles in the hidden
pockets of a life given over to remorse.
Sometimes startled by a mirror, the creak
of a floor or the hint of a perfume at the source
of a memory, the drifting soul will seek
out substance in anything just to assuage…
to bring another actor to the stage.

The Blue and the Yellow

A few yellow plum leaves show the wind
is down and the sky is dark and the days blow
into months then years. The clouds rescind
their flocks of starlings angling below
the sound of a jet all muffled in the tatters
around a single patch of blue. It's odd
how a moment buried in the past matters
less and less: the appointment missed, the wad
of cash we spent, the trip we took, the promise
we kept. A personal history seems so arch
among all the plans we hatch to calm us
for the future. Thus we practice our march
into the present, moving from day to day,
choosing the blue and the yellow over the gray.

Poor Rich Boys

Close the borders. Raise the fences. Others
are at the gates to infect us or bomb us or take
our jobs. What else is new? All the mothers
in the world don't have enough love to make
these poor rich boys safe. It's more of the same
ol' same ol' same. I know because I saw
it on T.V. Remember old what's his name?
The guy who was always trying to change the law
to make the future look more like the past?
The poor sonofabitch is crazy now
from years of consuming his own brain—
a *Reader's Digest* version of mad cow
disease. There's enough lead in his blood to line a
Walmart coffin (made by slaves in China).

Grounded

Those hoppers in the grass and in the ponds
blur the world between to something new.
What relief we take in broken bonds
turns the churning world a brilliant blue.
Take a colored pebble from a stream
and catch its hidden gleam before it dries.
Stay in bed a while; recall the dream
from which you just emerged. While wonder flies
we're grounded in the facts, the day to day
that makes it seem our days will never end;
then stunned we realize what's passed away
and find our lives have gone around the bend.
Without this mundane life there'd be no song,
in short, no boring things to make us long.

Fruit Fly Roots

A fruit fly makes its winter pilgrimage
from garbage can to counter while its red
eyes tunnel through the human sphere to dredge
up ancient imagery from its bed
of Neolithic fodder. Generations
ago such star stuff flew a straighter path
beyond all knowing into the many stations
rotting fruit demands. To do the math
we must consider what towering beasts
disturbed their tiny orbits now compressed
to those in atoms of coal. Consult the priests
of reason if you would count as blessed
the bloodlines of all who'd live and die,
just to arrive at last at this single fly.

While We Last

Like birds announce themselves to gravity
and flowers squander all they have on sex,
the windward world depends on brevity
and proffers every moment for the next.
To watch someone or something lose a life
requires a heart made out of sterner meat
than that which tries to reason with the knife
or find a life worth living in defeat.
When in dreams the dead return to us
and death has made them somewhat worse for wear,
as if to tell us not to make a fuss,
will we see our failed ambitions there?
If genomes tell the story of our past
let's celebrate that story while we last.

Coming to Grips

Here's to the limp handshake, the way we greet
each other when the oceans in us become
less deliberate and we feel the beat
common to all who add up to the sum
of an impending wave. A preacher learns
to grip the pulpit like a garbage can,
saving his gentler impulses for when he turns
to the myth of his public beliefs. Within the span
of a fly's life, the world can come to grips
with itself, pressing skin, scale, bone
and leaf into a micron of strata while ships
sail the gaze of those we've left alone
on the church's doorstep. One layer
after another we harden like an answered prayer.

Alive

We ride the dead as on a breaking wave,
poppies, flies and flounders, husbands and wives,
staking a future above a buffeting grave,
at one with a sliding web of tiny lives.
The *volvox* colony, the mastodon
buoying up our genes in valleys and peaks,
taking what preys and what's preyed upon
in stride with a shared sentience that seeks
out its kind, carrying extinctions like banners
in the chromosomes. Brother worm
and sister starfish, billions of wills, all manner
of shape and size, whether swimming sperm
or dormant seed, wave after wave we strive
toward the crest of the present, all alive.

A Simpler Language

My condolences to the living who totter
on the fulcrum of the dead. The breath,
latent in the wind, skims the water,
leaving evidence of another death
in riffles and tiny vortices. I've swallowed
my words like smooth pebbles, barely aware
of their significance. For all the hollowed
skulls that came before this attempt at prayer,
I contemplate the cryptic uses of the tongue,
knowing its sister muscle, the heart, speaks
a simpler language of the blood. When sung
in the throes of love or death, its song reeks
of roses and lilies and depends on the talents
of the living and all they hold in the balance.

Spaces

Snowflakes give dimension to the air
like schools of fish give water when they pass.
A sense of space seems more than we can bear
within our thoughts when random words amass.
The faces that we loved drift into view
then fade as we conceive apologies,
taking with them what we held as true
as brief as snow before the black of trees.
A blue *caesura* interrupts the song.
Do silences give gravity to voice?
Are any of us bound to be here long?
Do empty spaces cause us to rejoice?
A sky of stars disperses with the dawn.
We measure what is here by what is gone.

Crickets and Lilacs

Is love so silent and backward that it doesn't
have the will to recognize the sound
of flowers being picked for it? The pleasant
days love hid in the hedges, hanging around
just to hear its name called, were they wasted
on those swaggering couples, dressed to the nines
for a night on the town? Who hasn't tasted
rain as a child or recognized the signs
of an impending storm? To be left out,
to stand by an illuminated window
in the dark, is to experience the doubt
that brings love to light. This crescendo
of crickets and lilacs can turn a night to stone
in the memory of one who spent that night alone.

Dreary Purposes

Fresh from the morning's sacred garble, I
come dragging my dreary purposes. If roots
and stones would do their own bidding, why
usher them through this door that only suits
the needs of the dead? Walking down these sunny
sidewalks, I seldom notice the handprints
of children trapped in their youth. The money
in the wishing well will never convince
the little beggars of my lofty intentions.
The path into that final cave is slick
with mud. If I abandon the conventions
of my youth, will deer arrive to lick
sugar from my palm and birds land
on my finger wherever I might stand?

Lavish Funerals

Thanks to the bee's inventiveness, the world
becomes thicker, a place more for sex
than for prayer. When buds come unfurled
and hummingbirds crane their jeweled necks
to participate in the lavish funerals
accorded the humble, who will find the rigor
to put them all in their place? And what of the numerals
stamped on the butterfly's back? If hybrid vigor
animates the mishmash of the genes
into an arrow aimed at the future, then what
of the bow? Far from this morning of yellows and greens
comes the sound of the universe slamming shut.
Meanwhile back here, the spider, whale and pigeon
make of their bodies a perpetual religion.

An Edge

Out on winter's slippery tangent, flakes
in your headlights dazzle past the brights
hugging the car but never touching. It takes
a steady mind to navigate these whites
the road throws up as semis pass and all
the tragic outcomes splay the past into
a future blind as the night beyond the hall
your beams make down the road. If you
pull over, stop and kill the lights, you enter
such a privacy and stillness that
you find an edge to what was once a center.
Button your coat, pull down your hat,
and stand for a few moments till you see
your breath and know how gentle death might be.

Waking Worlds

An ending in the dust of undiscovered
planets marks what life we know with cool
resolve. When that perfect beginning hovered
in the lexicons of space, another rule
was broken for the sake of our waking dust.
When we prick a finger, worlds evolve,
and our matter does what matter must.
You'd think it wouldn't take such great resolve
to keep such waking worlds from falling slack.
But all the chaos centered in a thought
can't help but call the frenzied atoms back.
We must let go of anything we're taught
and prepare ourselves for entropy
to be the nothing that will set us free.

Those Outside

A window on the blackness isn't that
for those outside. Where we see a reflection
they see only us, petting a cat
or a dog, confident in the single direction
of our gaze, knowing the day will illuminate
a life beyond the glass. Meanwhile those
who tread the night are free to contemplate
our little protected spaces and compose
themselves accordingly. Do the dead
see us this way, garnering what they can
of our light from their darkness and dread?
No, of course it's only our image we scan
there on the tranquil surface of the night,
or so we suppose from our little patch of light.

Hard and Cold

Where the river ducks its shelves of ice
and darkens like an avenue in snow
I've laid my line against the cold's advice
to feel the tug of something down below.
It's more like dreaming than the other times
I wade the water searching for a clue
in places where the summer river climbs
down the rocks in shattered sheets of blue.
There seems to be a life beyond all reason
like that encountered in the pools of sleep
living hard and cold despite the season
in a realm as strange as it is deep.
So here's to all that's frozen, dark and dense
and to the mysteries found in difference.

The Plain Way

Out on the margins, the whale provides room
for a lack of mind. Such a vast blankness
relieves the microbes of the sudden doom
that rises from the cosmos in the thankless
act of procreation. Nothing is like
anything else, so why turn the telescope
one way or the other? Why try to psych
each other out with despair or hope
when the leaf scraping against the pane
foretells nothing but its own fall?
There is such radiance in the plain
way sun hits water why should we call
for the miraculous? Let heaven pass.
A blade of grass is just a blade of grass.

The Farmyard

The farmyard was a stirring green from all
the small deaths it took to keep the place
running. I can still hear Grandmother call
the cats from her bed in the nursing home, her face
animated by all the chores that she
was still doing in her head. In an attic
somewhere, her faded bonnet rests, free
of the sun among the drifting motes, a static
reminder with no one to remind. Walking
out among the chatter of sparrows, I think
of the barn, long since flattened, consigned to stalking
cats called home by nothing but the stink
of an empty wind. There's a dark green
in those shadows, much more felt than seen.

Filthy Fops

No matter where one finds the blue-bottle
and green-bottle flies, there's always some confusion.
Laid like jewels or courting Aristotle,
they buzz between what's real and what's illusion.
Close up their glimmer's framed by coarse black hair.
What fascinates us also makes us gag,
not unlike what makes *us* foul and fair.
Can beauty not exist without some snag?
They're such a jumbled knot of sex and death
tasting first the sky and then the soil,
sucking up what makes us hold our breath
then shining brightly like a piece of foil.
Without them life might be a dreary scene
denied those filthy fops to keep it clean.

A Spade

I've just read another free verse poem
about how the simple and pure can't be expressed
with rhythm and rhyme. To get down in the loam
and dig potatoes you need to get messed
up; it doesn't hurt to use your hands.
Down here on your knees for a purpose, you'll smell
the power that makes things grow. Nothing stands
for anything else once you're under the spell.
It helps to have a dog around to let
you know you're not alone in this tussle
with the tangible. And don't forget
the worms, the offhand way they twist and muscle
the soil aside. But then there's always the sort
who relies on a spade to cut everything short.

Doug

When I remember Douglas batting at
a painting of a magpie, it's as if
I saw him reflected in a mirror that
was reflected in a mirror. A stiff
dose of his recent departure from this earth
shows up in little scratches on the couch.
Who knows what such a subtle life is worth?
A basket of toys? Catnip in a pouch?
His darkness shadows me, even in the night.
His absence draws my glance to where he was
in a house that empties when I flip the light
or reach while reading just to feel his fuzz.
Though he's gone, he's never too remote
as long as I find traces of his coat.

Tame Ones

I remember mean geese, the way
they chased and pecked, and figure they must have gotten
it from somewhere beyond the barnyard clay.
I've seen little kids act twice as rotten
to each other, strike a mother, then float
out on their beach toys just as sweet as they
can be. I've felt that peck myself, that note
struck to jar loose any feathers that say
the world is as it should be. What keeps us on
our toes doesn't always make us stronger.
Wild geese seem much gentler in the dawn
stretching out their necks from long to longer
as their rage gets taken down a notch.
It's the tame ones that you've got to watch.

To the Bone

That the dead are alive in our genes is not
figurative. Our lost relatives climb
the rope ladders toward their dot
on our chromosomes and in the rhyme
of our DNA are found again.
The corpses that we trail in dust and ashes
buoy us up beyond that great amen.
Their blood's ours after the body crashes.
Whether wren or slug or tree frog, the bits
of all that came before us make us home.
Though we might use prayer to keep our wits
about us, we wear our parents to the bone.
When we say they're never coming back,
we use their cells to say it; that's a fact.

Anodyne

Here's to the cheesy, the ill-advised art
of those who go for the flash and bubble that
draw us all to a surface. Taking part
in the sun-drenched leaves, the fuzzy little cat,
the babies who can't avoid their cheeks, we give
ourselves over to the sugar-coated
impulse. Who'd deny the ones who live
a represented life, who choose the bloated
hopes of childhood over those who'd make
of taste a bitter pill? Better the anodyne,
the chicken-fried, the downy winter flake,
the easy choice of Kool-Aid over wine.
Protect us from those things that make us think.
We'll take our bunnies fluffy, white and pink.

Now and Then

Who'd stray from dark to light then back again?
This downward motion only water knows.
To learn to live without her now and then
I watch the spirit move from bud to rose.
The pulse within her wrist goes minnow light,
a shadow dancing at the edge of day.
How many prayers must a stream recite
before a single petal drifts away?
If only moss could know me like a stone.
I've lived within these corners much too long.
Does it matter where the wind has blown?
What if I shouldn't recognize its song?
Just like a bird would live without a door,
I'd learn to live for light and little more.

Once Open

To leave a lighter song I asked the leaves
what is it to die and yet to live?
What stands unburnished when the fire receives
the tinder that our fragile bodies give?
I stared into the markings on a fish
and saw a life beyond the skin and scales
while from a nest a feather like a wish
showed me how the simplest logic fails.
Great God of nothing, grant me in my rhyme
a willingness to vanish into words.
I've never found an easy way to climb
beyond the pathos of a single bird.
For all the doors once open that have closed,
there may be more to this than we supposed.

Fair

What of the old body, skin like scaly
paper, a mind in the wrong room at the wrong
time? Perhaps the soul knows its daily
dose of sun and moon, dancing to a song
the arms and legs were never meant to handle.
The body repeats and repeats like a stuck bird
enchanting the young who live beside the scandal
of the old, no more the wiser for a word
of wisdom until the spring winds down and fall
settles into the bones. The highs and lows
of emotion become a drumming beyond a wall
of failing tissue. Those who once made shows
of the thoughtless barb, the ornaments of care,
tire of the struggle and settle for feeling fair.

See the Opus

Talk of art is always such malarkey
like sailing without wind and without sail.
Yet somehow phantom crickets crick their quirky
songs, and others answer without fail.
And who would dare to map a slug's intentions
under where the lovers' blanket's spread?
Do even monkeys suffer the inventions
springing from another monkey's head?
Following that ever-present carrot
the dreamy horse gets put before the cart.
Perhaps 'most any fool could teach a parrot
to recount the finer points of art.
See the opus. See the critics judge it.
See them operate within a budget.

Now and Near

For peace of mind I count the meadow's flowers
trading numbers for a finer loss,
so when the sunny days give way to showers
I'll have a finite way to know the cost.
Wave on wave the grass has reassured me
of places I've discovered in the wind
though I've never found a place that's cured me
of that loss to which my hopes were pinned.
But looking back at what I took for granted
it's hard to garner any sympathy.
What is it that a death makes so enchanted
and turns what was to what will never be?
Best to think of things both now and near
and tally up the flowers while they're here.

Forecasts

Those years we used to cluster round the phone—
long distance from a mom or dad or other,
somehow left us more apart and alone
than table talk did when we failed to bother
with forecasts of our coming separations.
Oh, gods of failed nostalgia, link me up
with the boredom of those mild occasions
when nothing in the household seemed abrupt
and fortune filled the air with simple tunes.
Can coffee in the morning stop the presses
and engineer a calm before the swoon
of vodka taken as the day progresses
replacing the haphazard with the numb
and blowing any plan to kingdom come?

Rust and Mud

Happy as a boy in rubble, I pounded
nails from old boards while cottonwoods
snowed their seeds around me. Nothing sounded
wrong in the songs of locusts that had the goods
on any swelling life with a shed shell.
In it for the long haul, I dug
for China in my waking dreams and fell
for any girl who'd dare to catch a bug
just to let it go. A denizen of rust
and mud, I dammed the urban trickles
flirting with tetanus and raising the dust
in abandoned sheds then flattening nickels
on railroad tracks where, hunkered in broken glass,
I'd sing to myself and wait for the trains to pass.

A Static Perch

To have a drone's-eye view on things, all
one needs are the proverbial cross-hairs
and a static perch, sort of a balloon crawl
across the skies of any country that bears
the scars of tragic happenstance. The silent
little poof that shows up on the screen
among the scurrying shapes isn't violent
so much as it is curious. The scene
in the control room, the buttons and the toggle
switches, can be replicated almost anywhere.
There's nothing on either end that would boggle
the mind of one who wasn't actually there.
Of course, what's collateral's anybody's guess
when you don't zoom in on the actual mess.

A Bubble

Here comes another bubble beneath
the rainbow-studded waterfall. It's a form,
if only temporary, that has some teeth
to it when it comes to toeing a norm.
So far, this bubble has teeth and toes
and perhaps has a convex reflection of you,
or at least your face spilling away from your nose.
Like everything else, a bubble must be true
to time and space. Perhaps that's why, for the child
in all of us, it's a necessary waste
to chase one, to possess a wet and wild
rendition of the world (if you've a taste
for that sort of thing) until it stops
and, owing to its limitations, pops.

False Starts

Who can forgive me for the birds I've hurt
on a boy's whim or on a highway? The sun
is blind to the day's blank page, and the dirt
is always busy redoing what it's undone.
With puffed feathers and drooping wing
the roadside robin turns his back on the traffic
that stunned him, waiting for some dangerous thing
to help him feign a natural death. Such graphic
scenes seem small as a bullet and hit the heart
with no less force for their size. I'd look to the laws
of mice and hawks were it not for the false starts
we all make at the brink of oblivion. We pause
and wonder what engenders such a fuss
as the little lives leak out of us.

Busy Lives

Even the squirrels have things to do, or perhaps
I should say especially the squirrels, bickering among
the forged and splattered shadows. Pastel scraps
of morning float the clouds toward what's been sung
by the green hedge's singers. The wheels revolve
on passing cars heading for everyone's business.
How strange it is of industry to solve
the riddle of genetics, to span the isthmus
of the next few minutes and send a squirrel around
a tree or aim a lover away from a bed.
Could it be that something so profound
as a purpose in life would turn out instead
to be a gyroscope in the hands of a monkey?
All these busy lives should be so lucky.

A Small Regime

From a jumble of orchids she pulls a figurine
crafted in that exotic climate where artisans
suffer under the strictures of despots. A scene
all too familiar gets played out where guardians
of the status quo fly bloody sheets
from hotel balconies. A parrot here,
a monkey there, palms along the streets
all fall away as a portly captain's sneer
takes precedence over a postcard-perfect dream.
But wait, what have we here? A little
shop, a shaky hand, a small regime
dedicated to the noncommittal,
tapping to the sound of sudden rain,
happy though the work might be in vain?

Strangely Dangerous

When we feel it in our teeth we know
that love has reached a stronger limit than
the bone. How vulnerable and how slow
the tongue seems once bitten in its little span
where words from the heart are cut short to spare
another the depth of what we fail to say.
Thus we carry our teeth around as on a dare
from destiny, strangely dangerous in a way,
the lips cloaking something reptilian while
the face arranges itself for companionship.
To go behind the anatomy of a smile
is to know what lies around that strip
we do our best to keep so clean and bright,
(though we deal a down and dirty bite).

Stones

Looking at an old calendar, all
of those appointments in a life
I didn't realize I was living, I recall
those old suns, those moons, the wife
who urged me on through seasons till she took
herself away one spring. The paper, purged
since then of urgent messages to book
myself into a crucial future, has submerged
the past so deeply that the numbers on
the pages might as well be stones. Now
the urgency seems limited to dawn,
when I wake half remembering some vow,
some scrawlings of my all-important schemes
I've made for days marked only in my dreams.

Rungs

The rungs on the ladder are worn with use but down
we go anyway into the well
where reflections live or die and the town
we come from diminishes into the sound of a bell
calling all the fallen out from their places
in the shadows. The wet stones smell like a church
down here, a ruined church, glazed like faces
in the rain. Somewhere beneath, toads lurch
from dream to dream inventing walls with hands
like those of babies. Some disproven god
touches his lips to a trace of water, commands
a swarm of gnats to shut up. Given the nod,
we set the explosives and start the grueling climb
back to our puny world of place and time.

The Whole Shebang

Why do I want to grab a chickadee,
hold it to my ear and get it to spill
the beans? The Crow did and just see
where it got them. Their little tongues tell
the weather, or at least the season. I,
like Roethke, put faith in the little guys,
but the little gals? Perhaps that's why
I'm stuck there in that April when skies
stayed gray and sleet dotted that lot
where my wife ended a winter that had
gone on too long. But I've still got
a while to go as do, I might here add,
the chickadees, who stay put for the whole
shebang, no matter how long, how cold.

Word to Word

The pen is such a wobbly fuse, a drain,
a stem, a slippery bridge on roads from then
to now. Encampments in the rain,
our poems get washed away by what has been.
How green and tall the grass grows when they're gone,
how ripe and fat the plums that we intend
for no one but ourselves. What a yawn,
the grave without a death to fill it. Bend
the light. Go ahead, I dare you. Stake
your life on little things, a wren, a snail,
a star reflected in a mountain lake.
To have and eat the cake before it's stale
we flit from word to word hoping the next
will sidestep what a former self expects.

Little Hands

In the crackle and static of laundry being
separated a ghost sometimes arises
and goes about its dreary business of seeing
the utility in spiritual matters. It rises
to the occasion of, say, an open door
or a settling of beams somewhere above
or beneath the solitary dweller. The more
rote the life, the more substantial the shove
of little hands imagined for a purpose
that can be defined by isolation.
See the cobweb rise and fall from surface
to surface with nothing but a certain station
of light to move it. It's not so much occult
as a mind with nothing to consult.

A Pretty Lack

Even in a tick there is a dirge,
in the sparrow, in the spreading moss.
Baffled by such passing, who would purge
the shaded forest of its gnats or toss
a breathing fish upon a bank? Unhinged,
the oyster's shell becomes a pretty lack,
a faded shade with which the clouds are tinged.
And who'd believe there is no turning back?
Deep in the striations of the shale
the harbingers of all we are reside,
and somewhere in between the ant and whale
a million versions of our selves have died.
All that's ever been is passing still,
the shadow of a cloud upon a hill.

Just Lazy

What does she upon her starry throne
think of what she's left in us together?
Of course she'd laugh in her special tone
and say that we're just lazy, that we'd rather
fall back on our shared memory of her
than try to explain her to some stranger.
Even here I do my best to cover
all the bases with abstractions, to arrange her
just so, but wind up with blah, blah, or you
know what I mean—which you do, and that,
of course, is the point. What we can't do
is the look, the flair of the nostrils, the bat
of the lashes, the roll of the eyes saying this is half
dead serious, or not—and then the laugh.

Something Less

In Argentina Americans shoot doves,
thousands of them, until their shoulders ache.
I asked one who had returned, who loves
to hear them hit the ground, for the sake
of conversation, who eats them? "Hell, I
don't know," he said, "the hogs I guess."
One minute the doves are in the sky,
the next minute, they are something less.
But where do they come from, all these birds
that blanket the ground in photographs
of Americans, happy beyond words,
kneeling among the little bodies? Perhaps
there's no end to them, just as there's
not one who shoots who actually cares.

Something Irish

What sun we'd fail to salvage, so stubborn with
its small dose of light, would light her hair,
would keep her the same, beyond the myth
a man would have her be. Who would dare
to write a poem to define her when her grace
is in her penchant to resist such things?
Perhaps there's something Irish in her face,
or in the skin beneath the gold that rings
her wrist, that refuses to be compromised
by the impetuous. When her voice gets low
and flat, the listener had best be apprised
that her beauty harbors, within its glow
of graciousness, an instinct to preserve
her own, a will that will not swerve.

A Rising Breeze

I am one of the voices across the lake.
You can hear me best in the summer when
the wind is still, your fire is out and you've been
asleep briefly. If you listen closely, I'll take
your dream under a surface of stars and make
of it a glass ornament. Perhaps I'll then
bring that ornament to life among men
and women of care and compassion. For the sake
of tranquility, I'll have them converse in songs
and whispers that become a rising breeze
in the tree tops. Remember how sleep longs
for its own kind? Well, that's how these
voices will fade in the necessary joy of dawn
then, like reflections under wind, be gone.

Swimmer

What swirls here goes deep and makes food
where currents meet—like this crayfish whose shell
is in me and in his shell his meat. I can tell
which rock will tumble and release a brood
of nymphs, and I will set myself to include
them in the way I swim. There is a smell
I know to be a hidden frog, and hell
can be a sound from any surface, a mood
that comes to my moving house and makes
it stand still. I see it winding through light
and shatter in the path of swimming snakes.
I taste it in a moving piece of night,
and then my blood belongs away from me.
I hear my heart: to be, to be, to be.

Fallen Angels

Does everything that makes a living take
a dying in its stead? All those snow
geese on that pit of acid, that burning lake
our myths taught us to fear, who would know
how real a thousand fallen angels struggling
there could make it? Is this our time and place,
my friend, a mile of us, a white river haggling
down the wind toward that simple trace
of blue, that disc of our demise? What a lure
was made to make the world seem new
each time a switch was flipped on copper wire.
And who would lead us now but one who'd sue
to keep himself on course toward the blight
that he dreams up while tweeting through the night?

A Naked Woman

So you spent another night trying to calm
your bear, holding his head gently just under
his ears? He must think something of the balm
you give or he wouldn't have sought out your tender
touch there at the edge of your bath. It seems
you've prepared for him, anointing yourself
with lotions as for a sacrifice. Do dreams
work like this—or is this something else?
Perhaps a promise that you've kept to steady
the violent, to soothe what could kill you till
it hesitates and you come to feel its heady
mix of love and death. Too much? But still…
I know, I know, it's best to leave it there:
a naked woman comforting a bear.

Halfway Lost

Getting halfway lost isn't half bad
for those who've seen a muddy woodland gulch
of elk taking it easy. And though it's sad
to know the road's nearby, a steady pulse
among the scolding squirrels can keep a soul
pleasantly out of whack. And if a fever
takes it to a brook to make it whole
again, follow the water between the beaver
dams until directions seem so useless
you'd rather sit than walk. Soon the spires
of lupine all around will leave you clueless
and on your back. Nothing here requires
your attention, except perhaps a cloud or two
drifting toward and then away from you.

Gasoline Rainbows

How many hooks have I left in the streams
where trout go about their business
of living in spite of them? Are their dreams
as quick as they are? If I were to undress,
to lay my habits aside and lie face down
on cold stones, might I be allowed
into their sleep once and for all? This clown
who isn't funny anymore would crowd
the quiet evening with questions, hoping
that they might sprout wings, but the trout
aren't buying it. The trout are tired of coping
with gasoline rainbows. They want out,
and who would blame them? Is it really fair
that they should lose their colors on the air?

An Emerald Door

Here we are in this world where few people
know our names. How bright the sun, the moon
in the memory of water. How cold the ripple
that carries it out to an edge where lives resume
their chores in spite of the dead. And why would
a connoisseur of ceilings stare at a floor?
Out among the thunderheads where something good
might come of our dust, there is an emerald door
to that which we deny ourselves. Down here
among the gray partitions, the greater our
esteem for others, the more we have to fear
within ourselves. And though our eyes might scour
another's face for mercy, we settle for a sleep
more precious than our sentiments are deep.

The River

I called the river light, and it left me as fast
as it could. I called the river wind
and it laughed in my ears. I bid the river last
and it fell apart before my eyes. Chagrined,
I left the river to its own devices,
but it followed me at night among
the stars. I told the river about my crisis,
and it held the moon until I held my tongue.
I tasted the river in my tears and it turned
into an ocean. I held the river in
my arms where it struggled until I learned
the paths of my blood. I saw the river spin
a leaf and realized the futility
of fathoming the past for what will be.

Only the Moon

There he goes, making a joke of the moon
for her though she loves the moon. She would take
it to bed if she could, but he would make a balloon
of it and release it unknotted to sputter and shake
down to an empty thing. All the moonflowers,
moon fish and moon moths would follow her into her dreams,
while in his he'd explore the moon for its towers
of rock, more ample than its dust and beams.
Is he the poet and she the poem, or is it
the other way around? Perhaps it doesn't
matter, for all the dreams we visit
will never attest to whatever was or wasn't.
In the end it's all for love, so let's assume
they love each other, and the moon is only the moon.

Another Noise

Does it matter where the ashes go?
I've had them for so long, I'm starting to think
night is just another place to tote
this black trash bag of photographs. No one
would get it, so I dump everything
in the basement except the sheet music
from which she played show tunes. Weeping
is another noise I heard her make
before I knew what was happening.
There were just too few people there
for it to be anything but a mistake.
What a crazy sight it must have seemed
to those who watched us with our baggage.
A few charities still send her mail.

Except Your Mind

Lacking a flair for tragedy, your spitting
image wrests the mirror away from you
and drops it in a meadow where, wetting
itself among trout and beaver and all the blue
sky you've failed to imagine, it bids you to drink.
When you do, the red of rosehips stipples
the sky behind you all the way to the brink
of the pool as bright as aspens tinting the riffle
gold. Now that you've become electric
and swollen with color, you tilt an ear
toward the little gods buzzing their concentric
hymns in the air around you. Nothing's clear
except your mind that's given up and turns
itself to the tasks of flowers and ferns.

A Simple Tune

Say that on the hour that you were born
something casual issued from the night,
a simple tune played mellow on a horn:
"Cherry Pink and Apple Blossom White."
Say that all the seconds in between
have been measured by your beating heart
as the weather turns to white from green
and plans seem only made to fall apart.
Funny how the music and the flowers
become a fantasy for which we long
while the petty world around us sours
as if our hearts had never known the song.
But as the beauty stays in bloom and bud,
the music's always there; it moves our blood.

A Two-Note Song

Let the wind turn the pages and the writing
remain in longhand. I've given up trying to find
the right word for you. It's like biting
a chunk out of a rainbow. Or trying to bind
a hummingbird to its shadow. When you said
chickadee weather the air filled with the whir
of wings and a two-note song. Nothing's dead
after all. The snow was just a joke to stir
things up among those runty angels that stick
it out from white to green then back again.
How many histories have we shared to trick
ourselves? If we named one love would we then
be subject to the whims of birds, the blank slates
of yearly snows? There are worse fates.

One World

I heard you visited a fish briefly
when it rose to take a fly, a real fly,
not one of those constructed chiefly
out of spite for the real world. Try
as I might, I can't picture things when
there's any more than one world involved.
Sometimes I think you think I haven't been
standing in the river enough. That I've walled
it all into an aquarium with a plaster
mermaid who looks like my mother but, of course,
isn't. Any more it's hard to tell the caster
from the cast. Not that I'd endorse
one or the other. But honestly I wish
that I'd been with you when you saw that fish.

Like Darkness

I thought the owl was part of the tombstone, but
it was just an owl standing there,
probably looking for squirrels. It opened and shut
its eyes and swiveled its head to where
I couldn't see them anymore. It didn't
feel the need to fly I guess. Maybe
daylight is like darkness to owls. Hidden
behind its head that way, there in a shady
corner of the graveyard, I felt somehow
important, like you do when someone stupid
asks you a question and you raise an eyebrow.
I'm sorry if I'm not being particularly lucid,
but, you see, I'm used to being alone,
and it's not like that owl was set in stone.

Black Water

Sometimes in the woods the water looks
black where it pools near roots or mats of leaves
and needles. I have followed so many brooks
through so many meadows my blood conceives
of little but its dance with gravity.
And here comes the wind again, not much
but enough to give some levity
to the April snow. Are we so out of touch
with the dead? The muscle of the heart
stirs in its water. It would stop if it could,
but lightening keeps flashing, playing its part,
giving us nerve to remember the good
the dead do us—still. They still matter
in our veins till we ourselves fall to black water.

A Pleasant Confusion

The river as seen from a raft thereon would seem
to swallow the landscape whole, would tilt and wobble
those inside over the buckle of rapids and green
stretches of summer pools. And if we should bobble
our drinks and spill ourselves into the mood of the thing,
there's nothing in boulders sliding away or the hiss
and suck of eddies that wouldn't forgive us and sing
us through the slap of wavelets. Spun in a mist
of the river's devising, who wouldn't lose track
of the wind and clouds? Who wouldn't suffer the buffet
of gentle storms to join the flotillas of ducks
and mergansers, the pelicans dipping their ruffled
wings while herons wade and crane their necks
to see beyond the reflections? A pleasant confusion
takes us to shore where our minds are still moving.

A Fawn

I've followed the cottonwoods into their welter
of vines and mushrooms just to get at the heart
of water. Don't tell me it's gone, that the shelter
I felt there would fade in a swirl, would fall apart
in tufts on a breeze. Praise to the stagnant, the cove
in exposed roots. Let the rocks clatter down
around me. Let the muck pull me into the grove
and its shadows. If you find me curled, a fawn
in hiding, don't part the long grasses to see
how frail the shade has made me. I'm one
with the thistles and pods till a dream sets me free,
till the larvae tickle me senseless and the sun
wrestles its way down to the lichens and ferns
till the mother who left me returns.

In Nomine Patris

Of him I speak who, knowingly, rutted his way
away from death until (give me strength)
his sad fortune fell to, well, the gray
provinces of The Big C. Such angst
felt he that he had dug for him his own
cubic hell, away from tornadoes and bombs
there to study the Realists while the blown-
away world above (such were his many qualms)
continued to the tune of a distant carillon.
In nomine Patris I tweet from a device many
years beyond his early demise. Vermillion
knows little his veins except in mine, the plenty
of which subsides year by year yet stirs
me still. These lines, old ghost, not mine but yours.

Henry on the Potomac

Henry's not me. He's my grandson, my link
to all things Henry: those killer instincts
I wasn't allowed to see in myself, but did
anyway. The slide down which he slid
landed him on the Potomac among a wealth
of hills and forests. Lucky Henry, except
perhaps for Henry's double in fun and stealth,
Mr. Not So Much. He, too, crouched and leapt
out on a limb over the rush of the river.
And why not? It was the river that brought
him there. For what good reason would he sever
himself from all that stuff he loved? Okay, not
stuff, people. Henry, I'm too old
for this. The water's too deep, too cold.

Declensions

Could it be that here, in the folds of your
attention, I might rise to something other,
colder, more distant than the clouds that settle
on the mountains near our town? When
you said, "I'm old," I noticed in your voice
an evenness to match the slow and steady
rhythm of the heart. To be alone yet not
takes practice, like the trees that retrieve
their souls and shed their leaves to get them through
the winter. Have you known them all along,
the simplified declensions of a language
spoken only by the shy and quiet,
seldom asking why or to what end?
I hope that I am learning it, my friend.

Bluebird

He gives thanks for his security blanket,
without which the world would leave him bare.
It's blue, light blue, and no one knows he has it
but you. I'm not being cute, Bluebird, (Where
have you heard that before?) these boxes that
we huddle in beat being left to small
hawks. Right? So here's the deal: (What
am I thinking?) Just keep this raggedy doll
warm with your springtime wings. Okay?
I saw you trailing a horse above Ennis
for miles. I envy you your pain the way
you envy the color of the sky. When is
it? April? Cloud shadows? Enough sun to warm
a bird's blood and color her cover, her charm?

Additional titles from Elk River Books

Unearthing Paradise:
Montana Writers in Defense of Greater Yellowstone
edited by Marc Beaudin, Max Hjortsberg & Seabring Davis
foreword by Terry Tempest Williams

Vagabond Song:
Neo-Haibun from the Peregrine Journals
by Marc Beaudin
foreword by William Heyen

'or more information, please visit: ElkRiverBooks.com/press

d
:d
ry
an
ni-

About the Author

Greg Keeler has published two memoirs, *Waltzing with the Captain: Remembering Richard Brautigan* (Limberlost Press) and *Trash Fish: a Life* (Counterpoint Press). *Almost Happy* (Limberlost) is his latest of seven collections of poetry. He illustrated Jim Harrison's chapbook, *Livingston Suite*, NPR's *Car Talk* aired his song "WD-40 Polka," and Garrison Keillor read his poetry on three segments of *The Writer's Almanac*. He lives in Bozeman where he taught in the English department at Montana State University from 1975 through 2014.

Additional titles from Elk River Books

Unearthing Paradise:
Montana Writers in Defense of Greater Yellowstone
edited by Marc Beaudin, Max Hjortsberg & Seabring Davis
foreword by Terry Tempest Williams

Vagabond Song:
Neo-Haibun from the Peregrine Journals
by Marc Beaudin
foreword by William Heyen

For more information, please visit: ElkRiverBooks.com/press